Classic Cars of Havana, Cuba

A TRAVEL PHOTO ART BOOK

LAINE CUNNINGHAM

Classic Cars of Havana, Cuba

A Travel Photo Art Book

Published by Sun Dogs Creations
Changing the World One Book at a Time
Print ISBN: 978-1-951389-11-6

Cover Image by Laine Cunningham
Cover Design by Angel Leya

Copyright © 2023 Laine Cunningham

All rights reserved. No part of this book may be reproduced in any form or by any means, electronic, mechanical, digital, photocopying or recording, except for the inclusion in a review, without permission in writing from the publisher.

With an estimated 60,000 vintage cars on its streets, Cuba presents living, moving bits of history on every block. Classic American Fords and Chevrolets run alongside Soviet-era Ladas.

During the decades-long import ban, citizens repaired the autos that had already arrived in the country. Then, in the 1990s, the island's tourism industry boomed again. The cars that had been maintained for practical reasons suddenly grabbed attention.

A small number were exquisitely restored for the high-end touring trade. Many more became taxis, both those hailed through apps and those hailed with hand signals from the street.

Enjoy the lime-green, pink, and sky-blue classics cruising past Spanish Colonial buildings and through Havana's neighborhoods.

AOOGA

LAUNCH

WATCHDOG

LUX NEON

PASTURE

PALS

ATOMIC

GATED

CREAMY

IMPOSING

CUPCAKE

JOURNEY

DIMPLE

COORDINATED

POSTMODERN

MERLOT

YACHT

WINGS

WINK

JAM

RACETRACK

BULLSEYE

FILLED

SHOCK

SWOOP

VAMPIRE

SLICK

JAPANDI

GATHERING

ELEMENTAL

TBD

RUSH HOUR

LOLLIPOP

CABOOSE

QUARK

SHELLACK

DISTINGUISHED

PICNIC

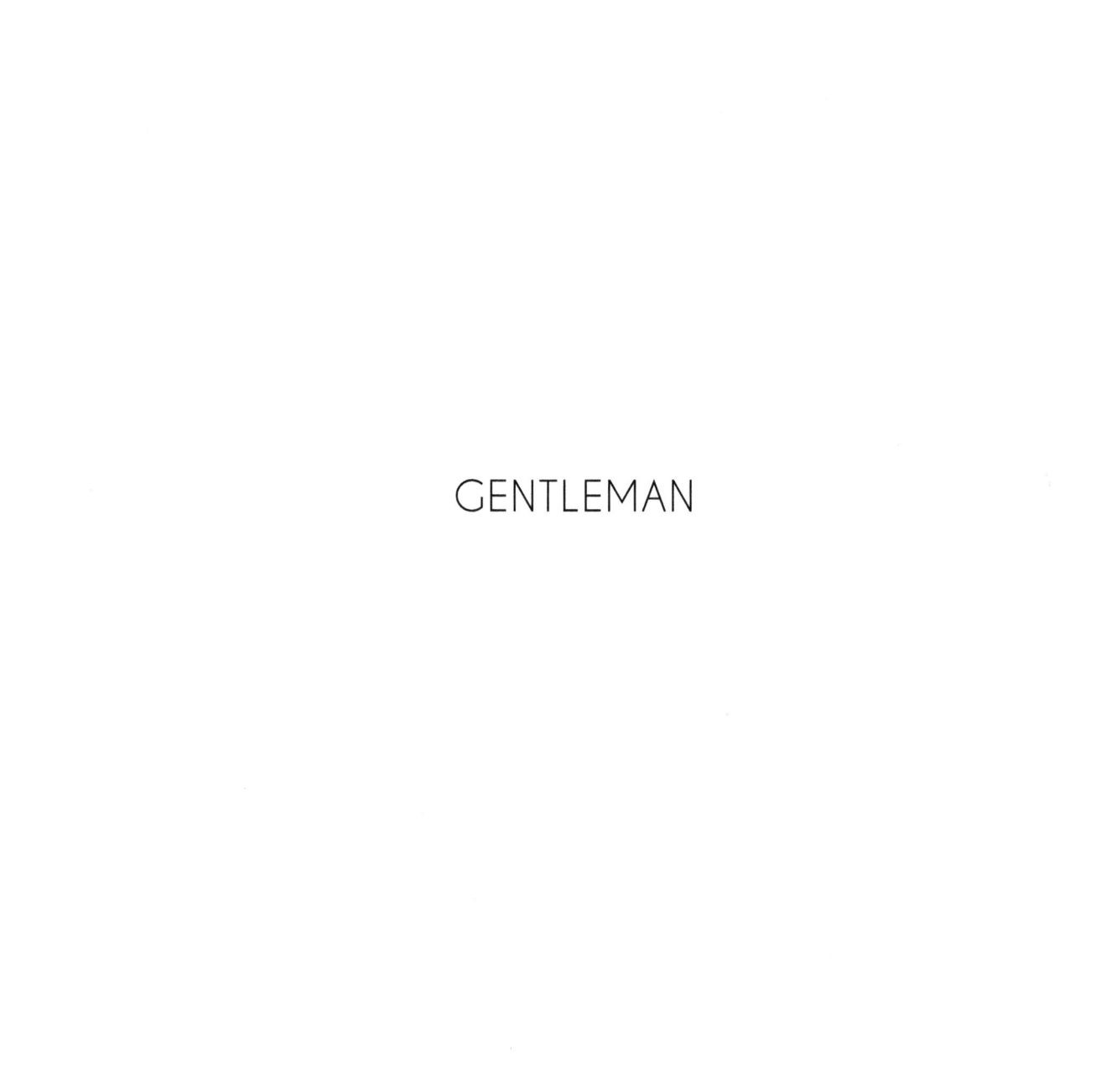

GENTLEMAN

LUCKY

SMOKING

GIBRALTAR

HOODWINK

WHOA

TITLES IN THIS SERIES

Havana, Cuba
Old Havana, Cuba
The Malecon, Havana, Cuba
Central Havana, Cuba
Vedado, Havana, Cuba
Regla, Havana, Cuba
Miramar, Havana, Cuba
Streets of Havana, Cuba
Classic Cars of Cuba
Classic Cars of Old Havana, Cuba
Classic Cars of Havana, Cuba
Spanish Colonial Havana, Cuba
Gardens of Havana, Cuba
Verge Gardens of Havana, Cuba
Cats of Havana, Cuba

www.ingramcontent.com/pod-product-compliance
Lightning Source LLC
Chambersburg PA
CBHW040001080526
44586CB00027B/2845